absolutely AFGHANS

Adorn your home with one of these gorgeous classic afghans and experience the feel of luxury that can only truly be found when using Caron® Simply Soft® yarn. The combination of this sumptuous yarn and these stunning designs will have your friends and family dropping hints for a wrap of their own!

Leisure Arts, Inc.
Maumelle, Arkansas

BASKETWEAVE THROW

FINISHED SIZE:
45" x 59"
(114.5 cm x 150 cm)

MATERIALS
Caron® Simply Soft® **MEDIUM 4**
[6 ounces, 315 yards
(170 grams, 288 meters) per
skein]:
Color A (#9742 Grey
Heather), Color B (#9707 Dark
Sage) and Color C (#9738
Violet) - 3 skeins of **each** color
Crochet hook, size I (5.5 mm)
or size needed for gauge

GAUGE SWATCH:
$2^3/_8$" (6 cm) square
Work same as Corner Square.

CORNER SQUARE
With Color B, ch 4; join with
slip st to form a ring.

Rnd 1 (Right side)**:** Ch 3
**(counts as first dc, now and
throughout)**, 2 dc in ring,
(ch 2, 3 dc in ring) 3 times, hdc
in first dc to form last ch-2 sp:
12 dc and 4 ch-2 sps.

Note: Loop a short piece of
yarn around any stitch to mark
Rnd 1 as **right** side.

Rnd 2: Ch 3, 2 dc in last ch-2 sp
made, ch 1, ★ (3 dc, ch 2, 3 dc)
in next ch-2 sp, ch 1; repeat
from ★ 2 times **more**, 3 dc in
same sp as first dc, ch 2; join
with slip st to first dc, finish off:
24 dc and 8 sps.

Note: Following the Placement
Diagram, page 5, make the
Squares in the color indicated.

ADDITIONAL SQUARES
Note: The method used to
connect the Squares is a
no-sew joining also known as
"join-as-you-go". After the
Corner Square is made, each
remaining Square is worked
through Rnd 1, then crocheted
together as Rnd 2 is worked.

With next color, ch 4; join with
slip st to form a ring.

Instructions continued on page 4.

Rnd 1 (Right side)**:** Ch 3, 2 dc in ring, (ch 2, 3 dc in ring) 3 times, hdc in first dc to form last ch-2 sp: 12 dc and 4 ch-2 sps.

Note: Mark Rnd 1 as **right** side.

Rnd 2 (Joining rnd)**:** Using Placement Diagram as a guide, work One or Two Side Joining.

ONE SIDE JOINING

Rnd 2 (Joining rnd)**:** Ch 3, 2 dc in last ch-2 sp made, ch 1, (3 dc, ch 2, 3 dc) in next ch-2 sp, ch 1, 3 dc in next ch-2 sp, ch 1; holding Squares with **wrong** sides together, sc in corresponding ch-2 sp on **previous Square**, 3 dc in same sp on **new Square**, sc in next ch-1 sp on **previous Square**, 3 dc in next ch-2 sp on **new Square**, sc in next ch-2 sp on **previous Square**, ch 1, 3 dc in same sp on **new Square**, ch 1, 3 dc in same sp as first dc, ch 2; join with slip st to first dc, finish off.

TWO SIDE JOINING

Rnd 2 (Joining rnd)**:** Ch 3, 2 dc in last ch-2 sp made, ch 1, 3 dc in next ch-2 sp, ch 1; holding Squares with **wrong** sides together, sc in corresponding

ch-2 sp on **previous Square**, † 3 dc in same sp on **new Square**, sc in next ch-1 sp on **previous Square**, 3 dc in next ch-2 sp on **new Square**, sc in next ch-2 sp on **previous Square**, ch 1 †, sc in next ch-2 sp on **next previous Square**, repeat from † to † once, 3 dc in same sp on **new Square**, ch 1, 3 dc in same sp as first dc, ch 2; join with slip st to first dc, finish off.

EDGING

Rnd 1: With **right** side facing and working in Back Loops Only unless otherwise instructed *(Fig. 1, page 32)*, join Color A with sc in second ch of any corner ch-2 *(see Joining With Sc, page 32)*; sc in next 3 dc, sc in next ch and in next 3 dc, ★ † sc in side of joining sc and in next 3 dc of next Square, sc in next ch and in next 3 dc †, repeat from † to † across to next corner ch-2, sc in next ch, ch 2, (sc in next ch and in next 3 dc) twice; repeat from ★ 2 times **more**, then repeat from † to † across to same corner as joining, sc in next ch, hdc in first sc to form last corner ch-2 sp: 644 sc and 4 corner ch-2 sps.

Rnd 2: Ch 1, sc in last corner ch-2 sp made, ch 1, skip next sc, ★ (sc in next sc, ch 1, skip next sc) across to next corner ch-2 sp, (sc, ch 2, sc) in corner sp, ch 1, skip next sc; repeat from ★ 2 times **more**, (sc in next sc, ch 1, skip next sc) across to first corner ch-2 sp, sc in first corner sp, hdc in first sc to form last corner ch-2 sp.

Rnd 3: Ch 5, dc in last corner ch-2 sp made, ★ (dc, ch 2, dc) in each ch-1 sp across to next corner ch-2 sp, dc in corner sp, (ch 2, dc in same sp) twice; repeat from ★ 2 times **more**, (dc, ch 2, dc) in each ch-1 sp across to first corner ch-2 sp, dc in first corner sp, ch 2; join with slip st to third ch of beginning ch-5.

Rnds 4 and 5: (Slip st, ch 6, dc) in next sp, (dc, ch 3, dc) in next sp and in each sp around; join with slip st to third ch of beginning ch-6.

Finish off.

Design by Martha Brooks Stein.

PLACEMENT DIAGRAM

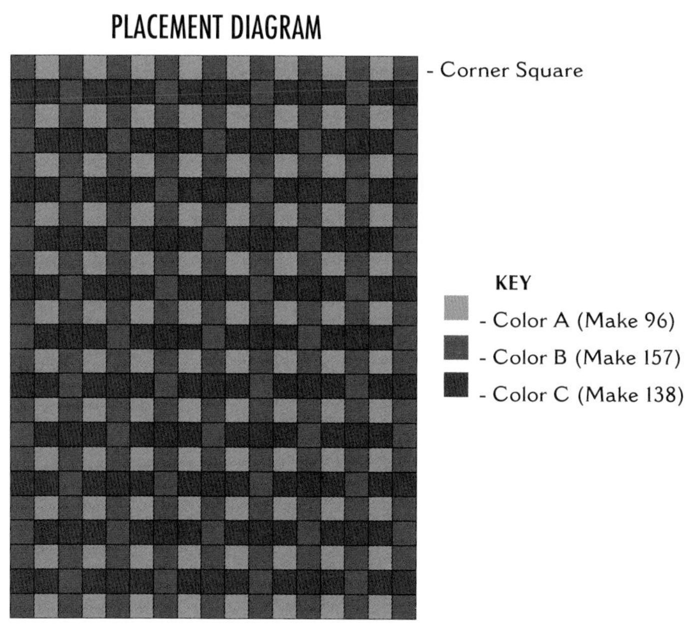

GRANNY SQUARE AFGHAN

■■□□ EASY

FINISHED SIZE:
37" x 50¹/₂"
(94 cm x 128.5 cm)

MATERIALS
Caron® Simply Soft® **4** MEDIUM
[6 ounces, 315 yards
(170 grams, 288 meters) per
skein]:
 MC (#9727 Black) - 3 skeins
Color A (#9710 Country Blue),
Color B (#9738 Violet), Color
C (#9707 Dark Sage), Color
D (#9703 Bone), and Color E
(#9730 Autumn Red) - 1 skein
of **each** color
Crochet hook, size I (5.5 mm)
or size needed for gauge
Yarn needle

GAUGE SWATCH:
4¹/₂" (11.5 cm) square
Work same as Square.

Note: Colors are placed
randomly on the first 3 rounds
and MC is used for the last
round.

SQUARE (Make 88)
Rnd 1 (Right side)**:** With first
color, ch 4, 2 dc in fourth ch
from hook, ch 2, (3 dc in same
ch, ch 2) 3 times; join with
slip st to top of beginning ch-4,
finish off: 12 sts and 4 ch-2 sps.

Note: Loop a short piece of yarn
around any stitch to mark Rnd 1
as **right** side.

Rnd 2: With **right** side facing,
join second color yarn with dc
in any ch-2 sp *(see Joining With
Dc, page 32)*; (2 dc, ch 2, 3 dc)
in same sp, ch 1, ★ (3 dc, ch 2,
3 dc) in next ch-2 sp, ch 1;
repeat from ★ 2 times **more**;
join with slip st to first dc,
finish off: 24 dc and 8 sps.

Rnd 3: With **right** side facing,
join third color yarn with dc in
any corner ch-2 sp; (2 dc, ch 2,
3 dc) in same sp, ch 1, 3 dc in
next ch-1 sp, ch 1, ★ (3 dc, ch 2,
3 dc) in next ch-2 sp, ch 1, 3 dc
in next ch-1 sp, ch 1; repeat from
★ 2 times **more**; join with slip st
to first dc, finish off: 36 dc and
12 sps.

Instructions continued on page 8.

Rnd 4: With **right** side facing, join MC with dc in any corner ch-2 sp; ch 2, 3 dc in same sp, ch 1, (3 dc in next ch-1 sp, ch 1) twice, ★ (3 dc, ch 2, 3 dc) in next ch-2 sp, ch 1, (3 dc in next ch-1 sp, ch 1) twice; repeat from ★ 2 times **more**, 2 dc in same sp as first dc; join with slip st to first dc, finish off leaving a long end for sewing.

ASSEMBLY

Afghan consists of 8 vertical strips of 11 Squares each. Lay Squares out to determine their placement before joining them.

Join Squares together as follows:
Place two Squares with **wrong** sides together. Thread yarn needle with long end on front Square and beginning in second ch of first corner ch-2, sew through both pieces once to secure the beginning of the seam. Insert the needle from **front** to **back** through **both** loops on **both** pieces *(Fig. A)*,

★ insert the needle from **front** to **back** through next stitch and pull yarn through; repeat from ★ across ending in first ch of next corner ch-2.
Whipstitch strips together in same manner using MC.

Fig. A

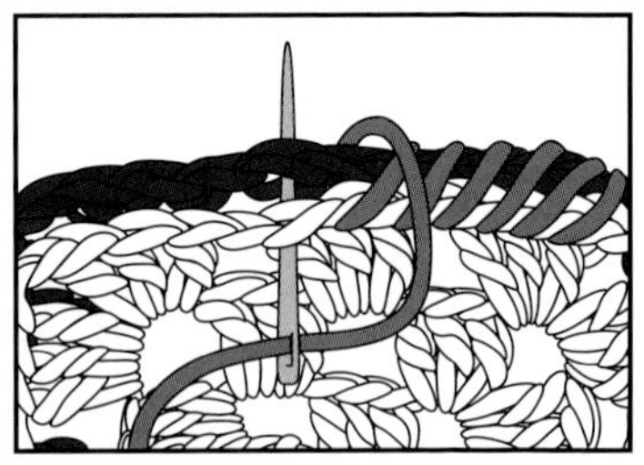

EDGING

With **right** side facing, join MC with dc in any corner ch-2 sp; (2 dc, ch 2, 3 dc) in same sp, ch 1, ★ (3 dc in next sp, ch 1) across to next corner ch-2 sp, (3 dc, ch 2, 3 dc) in corner sp, ch 1; repeat from ★ 2 times **more**, (3 dc in next sp, ch 1) across; join with slip st to first dc, finish off.

Design by Donna Childs.

WOODLAND MOTIF THROW

Shown on front cover & page 11.

FINISHED SIZE:
41" x 59"
(104 cm x 150 cm)

MATERIALS
Caron® Simply Soft® and Caron® Simply Soft® Heather
[6 ounces, 315 yards
(170 grams, 288 meters) per
skein **and** 5 ounces, 250 yards
(140 grams, 229 meters) per
skein]:
Color A (#9750 Chocolate),
Color B (#9707 Dark Sage),
Color C (#9503 Woodland
Heather), and Color D (#9502
Truffle Heather) - 2 skeins of
each color
Crochet hook, size I (5.5 mm)
or size needed for gauge

GAUGE SWATCH:
$4^{1}/_{2}$" (11.5 cm) diameter
Work same as First Motif.

Note: Beginning with
corner Motif indicated,
follow Placement Diagram,
page 13, referring to chart
below to make Motif with
colors indicated.

FIRST MOTIF
With color indicated for any
Motif, ch 5; join with slip st to
form a ring.

Rnd 1 (Right side)**:** Ch 3
**(counts as first dc, now and
throughout)**, 15 dc in ring;
with next color indicated on
chart, join with slip st to first dc
(Fig. A), cut old color: 16 dc.

Fig. A

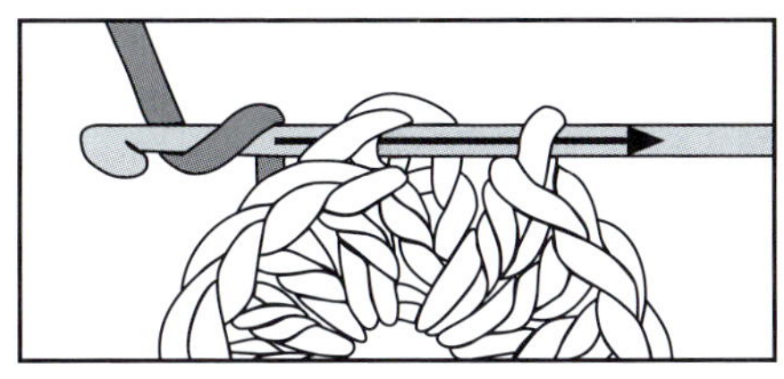

	Motif #1 (Make 28)	Motif #2 (Make 28)	Motif #3 (Make 28)	Motif #4 (Make 27)
Rnd 1	D	B	C	A
Rnds 2 & 3	B	D	A	C
Rnd 4	C	A	D	B
Rnd 5	A	C	B	D

Instructions continued on page 10.

Note: Loop a short piece of yarn around any stitch to mark Rnd 1 as **right** side.

Rnd 2: Ch 1, sc in same st as joining, ch 5, skip next dc, ★ sc in next dc, ch 5, skip next dc; repeat from ★ around; join with slip st to first sc: 8 ch-5 sps.

Rnd 3: Slip st in next ch-5 sp, ch 1, 4 sc in same sp and in each ch-5 sp around; with next color, join with slip st to first sc, cut old color: 32 sc.

Rnd 4: Ch 4 (**counts as first dc plus ch 1, now and throughout**), dc in same st as joining, skip next sc, ★ (dc, ch 1, dc) in next sc, skip next sc; repeat from ★ around; with next color, join with slip st to first dc, cut old color: 32 dc and 16 ch-1 sps.

Rnd 5: Slip st in next ch-1 sp, ch 3, 4 dc in same sp, sc in next ch-1 sp, (5 dc in next ch-1 sp, sc in next ch-1 sp) around; join with slip st to first dc, finish off: 8 5-dc groups.

ADDITIONAL MOTIFS

Note: The method used to connect the Motifs is a no-sew joining also known as "join-as-you-go". After the First Motif is made, each remaining Motif is worked through Rnd 4, then crocheted together as Rnd 5 is worked.

Work same as First Motif through Rnd 4: 32 dc and 16 ch-1 sps.

Rnd 5 (Joining rnd): Using Placement Diagram as a guide, work One or Two Side Joining.

ONE SIDE JOINING

Rnd 5 (Joining rnd): Slip st in next ch-1 sp, ch 3, 4 dc in same sp, sc in next ch-1 sp, (5 dc in next ch-1 sp, sc in next ch-1 sp) 5 times, ★ 2 dc in next ch-1 sp, drop loop from hook, with **right** side of **adjacent Motif** facing, insert hook in center dc of corresponding 5-dc group, pick up dropped loop and draw through center dc, 3 dc in same ch-1 sp on **new Motif**, sc in next ch-1 sp; repeat from ★ once **more**; join with slip st to first dc, finish off.

Instructions continued on page 12.

TWO SIDE JOINING

Rnd 5 (Joining rnd)**:** Slip st in next ch-1 sp, ch 3, 4 dc in same sp, sc in next ch-1 sp, (5 dc in next ch-1 sp, sc in next ch-1 sp) 3 times, ★ 2 dc in next ch-1 sp, drop loop from hook, with **right** side of **adjacent Motif** facing, insert hook in center dc of corresponding 5-dc group, pick up dropped loop and draw through center dc, 3 dc in same ch-1 sp on **new Motif**, sc in next ch-1 sp; repeat from ★ 3 times **more**; join with slip st to first dc, finish off.

Note: Following Placement Diagram, page 13, refer to chart below to make Half Motif indicated.

HALF MOTIFS

With color indicated for any Half Motif, ch 5; join with slip st to form a ring.

Row 1 (Right side)**:** Ch 3, 8 dc in ring changing to next color indicated on chart in last dc made *(Fig. B)*; cut old color: 9 dc.

Fig. B

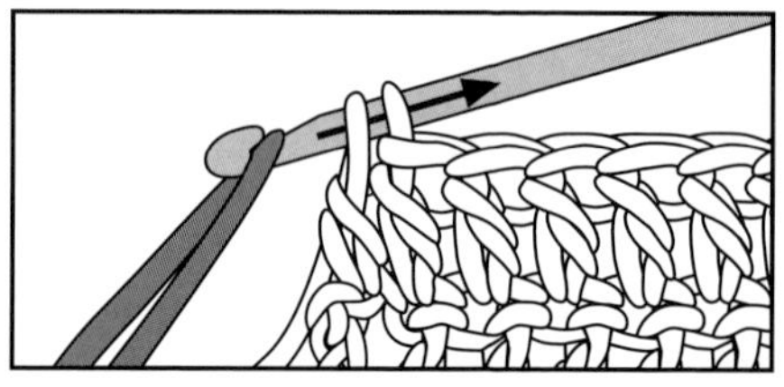

Note: Mark Row 1 as **right** side.

	Half Motif #1 (Make 3)	Half Motif #2 (Make 2)	Half Motif #3 (Make 3)	Half Motif #4 (Make 4)
Rnd 1	D	B	C	A
Rnds 2 & 3	B	D	A	C
Rnd 4	C	A	D	B
Rnd 5	A	C	B	D

Row 2: Ch 1, turn; sc in first dc, ★ ch 5, skip next dc, sc in next dc; repeat from ★ across: 4 ch-5 sps.

Row 3: Turn; slip st in next ch-5 sp, ch 1, 4 sc in same sp and in each of next 2 ch-5 sps, 5 sc in last ch-5 sp; finish off: 17 sc.

Row 4: With **right** side facing, join next color with slip st in first sc; ch 4, dc in same st, ★ skip next sc, (dc, ch 1, dc) in next sc; repeat from ★ across; finish off: 18 dc and 9 ch-1 sps.

Row 5 (Joining row): With **right** side facing, join next color with sc in first ch-1 sp *(see Joining With Sc, page 32)*; ★ 2 dc in next ch-1 sp, drop loop from hook, with **right** side of **adjacent Motif** facing, insert hook in center dc of corresponding 5-dc group, pick up dropped loop and draw through center dc, 3 dc in same ch-1 sp on **Half Motif,** sc in next ch-1 sp; repeat from ★ 3 times **more;** finish off.

Instructions continued on page 14.

PLACEMENT DIAGRAM

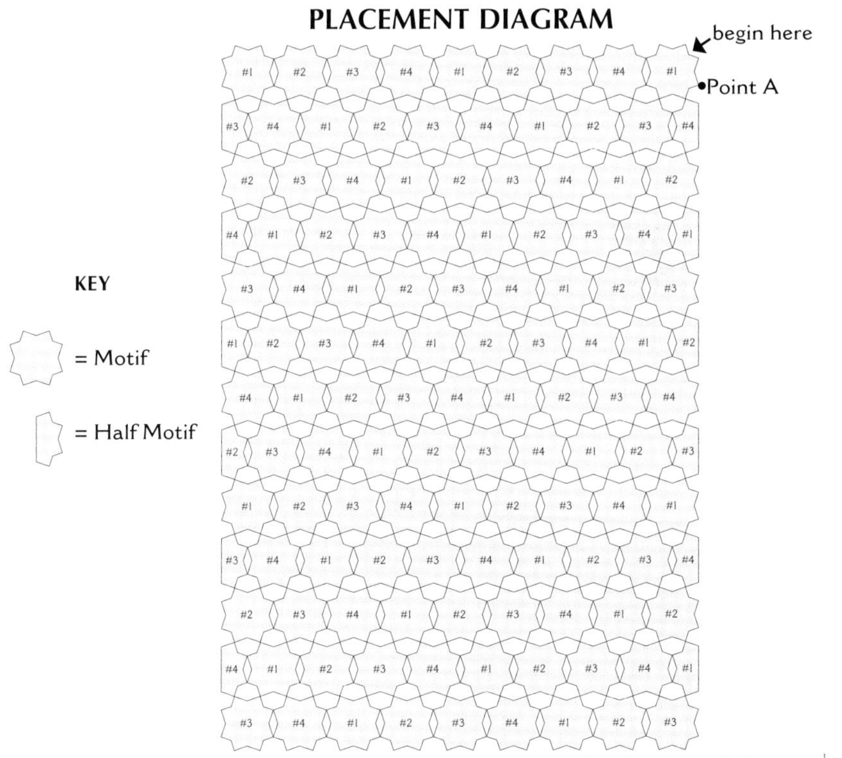

EDGING

To decrease (uses 2 joining dc), pull up a loop in joining dc on same Motif and in joining dc on next Motif, YO and draw through all 3 loops on hook **(counts as one sc)**.

Rnd 1: With **right** side facing, join Color A with sc in center dc of 5-dc group on First Motif (at Point A on Placement Diagram); sc in same st and in next 2 dc, ♥ skip next sc, sc in next 2 dc, [3 sc in next dc, sc in next 2 dc, skip next sc, sc in next 2 dc] 3 times, decrease, † sc in next 2 dc, skip next sc, sc in next 2 dc, [3 sc in next dc, sc in next 2 dc, skip next sc, sc in next 2 dc] twice, decrease †; repeat from † to † across to next corner Motif, sc in next 2 dc, skip next sc, sc in next 2 dc, [3 sc in next dc, sc in next 2 dc, skip next sc, sc in next 2 dc] 4 times, decrease, sc in next 2 dc, work 6 sc evenly spaced across end of rows on Half Motif to beginning ring, sc in beginning ring, work 6 sc evenly spaced across end of rows on same Half Motif, sc in next 2 dc, decrease, [repeat from † to † once, sc in next 2 dc, work 6 sc evenly spaced across end of rows on Half Motif to beginning ring, sc in beginning ring, work 6 sc evenly spaced across end of rows on same Half Motif, sc in next 2 dc, decrease] across to next corner Motif, sc in next 2 dc, skip next sc, sc in next 2 dc ♥, 3 sc in next dc, sc in next 2 dc, repeat from ♥ to ♥ once, sc in same st as first sc; join with slip st to first sc: 804 sc.

Rnd 2: Ch 1, sc in same st as joining, † (sc in next 6 sc, 3 sc in next sc) 3 times, sc in next 11 sc, 3 sc in next sc, [sc in next 6 sc, 3 sc in next sc, sc in next 11 sc, 3 sc in next sc] across to next corner Motif, (sc in next 6 sc, 3 sc in next sc) 3 times, sc in next 3 sc, skip next 2 sc, 5 dc in next sc, skip next 2 sc, (sc in next 4 sc, skip next 2 sc, 5 dc in next sc, skip next 2 sc) twice, [sc in next 3 sc, 3 sc in next sc, sc in next 6 sc, 3 sc in next sc, sc in next 3 sc, skip next 2 sc, 5 dc in next sc, skip next 2 sc, (sc in next 4 sc, skip next 2 sc, 5 dc in next sc, skip next 2 sc) twice] across to next corner Motif †, sc in next 3 sc, 3 sc in next sc, repeat from † to † once, sc in next 3 sc and in same st as first sc; join with slip st to first sc, finish off.

Design by Treva G. McCain.

KALEIDOSCOPE THROW

Shown on page 17.

Finished Size:
40¹/₂" x 56"
(103 cm x 142 cm)

MATERIALS
Caron® Simply Soft® **MEDIUM 4**
[6 ounces, 315 yards
(170 grams, 288 meters) per
skein]:
Color A (#9710 Country Blue)
- 3 skeins
Color B (#9703 Bone)
- 2 skeins
Color C (#9711 Dk Country
Blue) - 2 skeins
Color D (#9709 Lt Country
Blue) - 1 skein
Crochet hook, size I (5.5 mm)
or size needed for gauge
Yarn needle

GAUGE SWATCH:
7³/₄" (19.75 cm) square
Work same as Square through
Rnd 8.

STITCH GUIDE
TREBLE CROCHET
   (abbreviated tr)
YO twice, insert hook in st or
sp indicated, YO and pull up
a loop (4 loops on hook), (YO
and draw through 2 loops on
hook) 3 times.

DOUBLE TREBLE CROCHET
   (abbreviated dtr)
YO 3 times, insert hook in sp
indicated, YO and pull up a
loop (5 loops on hook), (YO
and draw through 2 loops on
hook) 4 times.

FIRST SQUARE
With Color A, ch 4; join with
slip st to form a ring.

Rnd 1 (Right side)**:** Ch 3
(counts as first dc), 15 dc in
ring; join with slip st to first dc,
finish off: 16 dc.

Note: Loop a short piece of
yarn around any stitch to mark
Rnd 1 as **right** side.

Rnd 2: With **right** side facing,
join Color D with dc in same
st as joining *(see Joining With
Dc, page 32)*; dc in same st,
ch 3, skip next 3 dc, ★ (2 dc,
ch 2, 2 dc) in next dc, ch 3,
skip next 3 dc; repeat from ★
2 times **more**, 2 dc in same st
as first dc, ch 2; join with slip st
to first dc, finish off: 16 dc and
8 sps.

Instructions continued on page 16.

Rnd 3: With **right** side facing and working **around** ch-3 *(Fig. A)*, join Color B with slip st in any center skipped dc on Rnd 1; ch 4 **(counts as first tr, now and throughout)**, tr in same st, ch 3, skip next ch-2 sp, ★ working **around** next ch-3, (2 tr, ch 3) twice in next center skipped dc on Rnd 1, skip next ch-2 sp; repeat from ★ 2 times **more**, 2 tr in same st as first tr, ch 3; join with slip st to first tr, finish off.

Fig. A

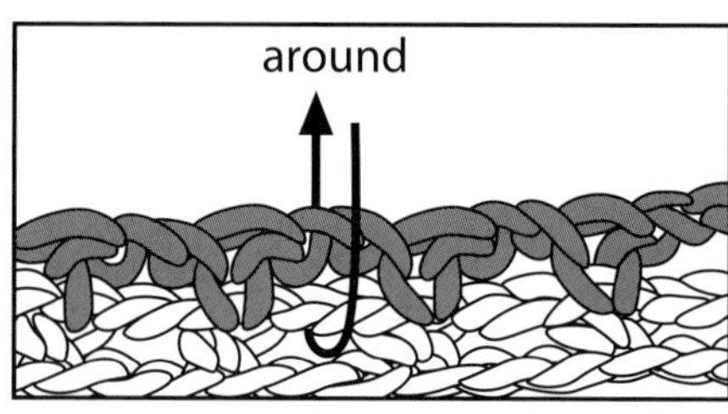

Rnd 4: With **right** side facing and working **around** ch-3, join Color A with slip st in any skipped ch-2 sp on Rnd 2; ch 4, 2 tr in same sp, ch 3, skip next ch-3 sp, ★ working **around** next ch-3, (3 tr, ch 3) twice in next skipped ch-2 sp on Rnd 2; repeat from ★ 2 times **more**, 3 tr in same sp as first tr, ch 3; join with slip st to first tr, finish off: 24 tr and 8 ch-3 sps.

Rnd 5: With **right** side facing and working **around** ch-3, join Color C with slip st in any skipped ch-3 sp on Rnd 3; ch 4, 3 tr in same sp, ch 3, skip next ch-3 sp, ★ working **around** next ch-3, (4 tr, ch 3) twice in next skipped ch-3 sp on Rnd 3; repeat from ★ 2 times **more**, 4 tr in same sp as first tr, ch 3; join with slip st to first tr, finish off: 32 tr and 8 ch-3 sps.

Rnd 6: With **right** side facing and working **around** ch-3, join Color B with slip st in any skipped ch-3 sp on Rnd 4; ch 5 **(counts as first dtr)**, 4 dtr in same sp, ch 4, skip next ch-3 sp, ★ working **around** next ch-3, (5 dtr, ch 4) twice in next skipped ch-3 sp on Rnd 4; repeat from ★ 2 times **more**, 5 dtr in same sp as first tr, ch 4; join with slip st to first dtr, finish off: 40 dtr and 8 ch-4 sps.

Instructions continued on page 18.

Rnd 7: With **right** side facing, join Color A with sc in any corner ch-4 sp *(see Joining With Sc, page 32)*; 2 sc in same sp, sc in next 5 dtr, working **around** next ch-4, 5 sc in next skipped ch-3 sp on Rnd 5, sc in next 5 dtr, ★ 7 sc in next corner ch-4 sp, sc in next 5 dtr, working **around** next ch-4, 5 sc in next skipped ch-3 sp on Rnd 5, sc in next 5 dtr; repeat from ★ 2 times **more**, 4 sc in same sp as first sc; join with slip st to first sc, do **not** finish off: 88 sc.

Rnd 8: Ch 1, **turn**; skip joining slip st, ★ (sc, ch 2, sc) in next sc **(corner made)**, ch 1, skip next sc, (sc in next sc, ch 1, skip next sc) 10 times; repeat from ★ around; join with slip st to first sc, finish off: 48 sc and 48 sps.

Rnd 9: With **right** side facing, join Color C with sc in any corner ch-2 sp; ch 2, sc in same sp, ch 1, (sc in next ch-1 sp, ch 1) 11 times, ★ (sc, ch 2, sc) in next corner ch-2 sp, ch 1, (sc in next ch-1 sp, ch 1) 11 times; repeat from ★ 2 times **more**; join with slip st to first sc, finish off: 52 sc and 52 sps.

ADDITIONAL SQUARES

Note: The method used to connect the Squares is a no-sew joining also known as "join-as-you-go". After the First Square is made, each remaining Square is worked through Rnd 8, then crocheted together as Rnd 9 is worked. If a corner has been previously joined, work new join into the slip st of the first join made.

Work same as First Square through Rnd 8: 48 sc and 48 sps.

Rnd 9 (Joining rnd)**:** Work One or Two Side Joining, arranging Squares into 5 vertical strips of 7 squares each.

ONE SIDE JOINING

Rnd 9 (Joining rnd)**:** With **right** side facing, join Color C with sc in any corner ch-2 sp; ch 1, (sc in next ch-1 sp, ch 1) 11 times, ★ (sc, ch 2, sc) in next corner ch-2 sp, ch 1, (sc in next ch-1 sp, ch 1) 11 times; repeat from ★ once **more**, sc in next corner ch-2 sp, ch 1; with **wrong** sides together, slip st in corresponding corner ch-2 sp on **previous Square**, ch 1, sc in same corner sp on **new Square**, slip st in next ch-1 sp on **previous Square**, ch 1, (sc in next ch-1 sp on **new Square**, slip st in next ch-1 sp on **previous Square**, ch 1) 11 times, sc in same corner sp on **new Square** as joining sc, ch 1, slip st in next corner ch-2 sp on **previous Square**, ch 1; join with slip st to first sc on **new Square**, finish off.

TWO SIDE JOINING

Rnd 9 (Joining rnd)**:** With **right** side facing, join Color C with sc in any corner ch-2 sp; ch 1, (sc in next ch-1 sp, ch 1) 11 times, (sc, ch 2, sc) in next corner ch-2 sp, ch 1, (sc in next ch-1 sp, ch 1) 11 times, sc in next corner ch-2 sp, ch 1; with **wrong** sides together, slip st in corresponding corner ch-2 sp on **previous Square**, † ch 1, sc in same corner sp on **new Square**, slip st in next ch-1 sp on **previous Square**, ch 1, (sc in next ch-1 sp on **new Square**, slip st in next ch-1 sp on **previous Square**, ch 1) 11 times †, sc in next corner ch-2 sp on **new Square**, ch 1, slip st in next corner ch-2 sp on **previous Square**, repeat from † to † once, sc in same corner sp on **new Square** as joining sc, ch 1, slip st in next corner ch-2 sp on **previous Square**, ch 1; join with slip st to first sc on **new Square**, finish off.

EDGING

Rnd 1: With **wrong** side facing, join Color C with sc in any corner ch-2 sp; ch 1, (sc in next sp, ch 1) 13 times, ★ † skip next joining, (sc in next sp, ch 1) 14 times †, repeat from † to † across to last Square, skip next joining, (sc in next sp, ch 1) 13 times, (sc, ch 2, sc) in next corner ch-2 sp, ch 1, (sc in next sp, ch 1) 13 times; repeat from ★ 2 times **more**, then repeat from † to † across; join with slip st to first sc, finish off.

Rnd 2: With **right** side facing, join Color A with slip st in any corner ch-2 sp; ch 1, working from **left** to **right**, ★ work reverse sc in next ch-1 sp *(Figs. 2a-d, page 32)*, ch 1; repeat from ★ around; join with slip st to first reverse sc, finish off.

Design by Doris Chan.

ROSE GARDEN THROW

◖◼◼◼◻ INTERMEDIATE

FINISHED SIZE: 43¹/₂" x 60"
(110.5 cm x 152.5 cm)

MATERIALS
Caron® Simply Soft® and Simply Soft® Brites
[6 ounces, 315 yards
(170 grams, 288 meters) per skein]:
Color A (#9722 Plum Wine) -
3 skeins
Color B (#9611 Rose Violet) -
3 skeins
Color C (#9707 Dark Sage) -
2 skeins
Color D (#9705 Sage) - 1 skein
Crochet hook, size I (5.5 mm)
or size needed for gauge

GAUGE SWATCH:
2³/₈" (6 cm) square
Work same as Corner Square.

CORNER SQUARE
With Color A, ch 4; join with slip st to form a ring.

Rnd 1 (Right side)**:** Ch 3
(counts as first dc, now and throughout), 2 dc in ring, (ch 2, 3 dc in ring) 3 times, hdc in first dc to form last ch-2 sp:
12 dc and 4 ch-2 sps.

Note: Loop a short piece of yarn around any stitch to mark Rnd 1 as **right** side.

Rnd 2: Ch 3, 2 dc in last ch-2 sp made, ch 1, ★ (3 dc, ch 2, 3 dc) in next ch-2 sp, ch 1; repeat from ★ 2 times **more**, 3 dc in same sp as first dc, ch 2; join with slip st to first dc, finish off: 24 dc and 8 sps.

Note: Following the Placement Diagram, page 23, make the Squares in the color indicated.

ADDITIONAL SQUARES
Note: The method used to connect the Squares is a no-sew joining also known as "join-as-you-go". After the First Square is made, each remaining Square is worked through Rnd 1, then crocheted together as Rnd 2 is worked.

With next color indicated on Placement Diagram, ch 4; join with slip st to form a ring.

Instructions continued on page 22.

Rnd 1 (Right side): Ch 3, 2 dc in ring, (ch 2, 3 dc in ring) 3 times, hdc in first dc to form last ch-2 sp: 12 dc and 4 ch-2 sps.

Note: Mark Rnd 1 as **right** side.

Rnd 2 (Joining rnd): Using Placement Diagram as a guide, work One or Two Side Joining.

ONE SIDE JOINING

Rnd 2 (Joining rnd): Ch 3, 2 dc in last ch-2 sp made, ch 1, (3 dc, ch 2, 3 dc) in next ch-2 sp, ch 1, 3 dc in next ch-2 sp, ch 1; holding Squares with **wrong** sides together, sc in corresponding ch-2 sp on **previous Square**, 3 dc in same sp on **new Square**, sc in next ch-1 sp on **previous Square**, 3 dc in next ch-2 sp on **new Square**, sc in next ch-2 sp on **previous Square**, ch 1, 3 dc in same sp on **new Square**, ch 1, 3 dc in same sp as first dc, ch 2; join with slip st to first dc, finish off.

TWO SIDE JOINING

Rnd 2 (Joining rnd): Ch 3, 2 dc in last ch-2 sp made, ch 1, 3 dc in next ch-2 sp, ch 1; holding Squares with **wrong** sides together, sc in corresponding ch-2 sp on **previous Square**,
† 3 dc in same sp on **new Square**, sc in next ch-1 sp on **previous Square**, 3 dc in next ch-2 sp on **new Square**, sc in next ch-2 sp on **previous Square**, ch 1 †, sc in next ch-2 sp on **next previous Square**, repeat from † to † once, 3 dc in same sp on **new Square**, ch 1, 3 dc in same sp as first dc, ch 2; join with slip st to first dc, finish off.

EDGING

Rnd 1: With **right** side facing, join Color C with dc in any corner ch-2 sp *(see Joining With Dc, page 32)*; dc in same sp and in next dc, ch 1, skip next dc, dc in next dc, dc in next ch-1 sp and in next dc, ch 1, ★ † skip next 2 dc, dc in next sp, dc in joining sc and in next sp, ch 1, skip next 2 dc, dc in next dc, dc in next ch-1 sp and in next dc, ch 1 †, repeat from † to † across to within 2 dc of next corner ch-2 sp, skip next dc, dc in next dc, (2 dc, ch 2, 2 dc) in corner sp, dc in next dc, ch 1, skip next dc, dc in next dc, dc in next ch-1 sp and in next dc, ch 1; repeat from ★ 2 times **more**, then repeat from † to † across to within 2 dc of first corner ch-2 sp, skip next dc, dc in next dc, 2 dc in same corner sp as first dc, hdc in first dc to form last corner ch-2 sp: 504 dc and 168 sps.

Rnd 2: Ch 3, dc in last corner ch-2 sp made and in next dc, ★ † ch 1, skip next dc, dc in next dc, (dc in next ch-1 sp and in next dc, ch 1, skip next dc, dc in next dc) across to next corner ch-2 sp †, (2 dc, ch 2, 2 dc) in corner sp, dc in next dc; repeat from ★ 2 times **more**, then repeat from † to † once, 2 dc in same corner sp as first dc, hdc in first dc to form last corner ch-2 sp.

Rnd 3: Ch 3, dc in last corner ch-2 sp made and in next dc, ★ † ch 1, skip next dc, dc in next dc, (dc in next ch-1 sp and in next dc, ch 1, skip next dc, dc in next dc) across to next corner ch-2 sp †, (2 dc, ch 2, 2 dc) in corner sp, dc in next dc; repeat from ★ 2 times **more**, then repeat from † to † once, 2 dc in same corner sp as first dc, ch 2; join with slip st to first dc.

Rnd 4: Ch 1, working from **left** to **right** *(Figs. 2a-d, page 32)*, ★ (sc, ch 3) twice in next corner sp, (sc in center dc of next 3-dc group, ch 3) across to next corner ch-2 sp; repeat from ★ around; join with slip st to first sc, finish off.

Design by Martha Brooks Stein.

- Corner Square

PLACEMENT DIAGRAM

KEY

- Color A (Make 165)
- Color B (Make 158)
- Color C (Make 51)
- Color D (Make 34)

SOLID COLOR MOTIF THROW

EASY

FINISHED SIZE:
41" x 51¹/₄"
(104 cm x 130 cm)

MATERIALS
Caron® Simply Soft® **MEDIUM 4**
[6 ounces, 315 yards
(170 grams, 288 meters) per
skein]:
#9702 Off White - 6 skeins
Crochet hook, size H (5 mm)
or size needed for gauge

GAUGE:
13 sc and 20 rows = 4" (10 cm)
One Square (before edging) =
9" (22.75 cm) square

Gauge Swatch: 4" (10 cm)
square
Work same as Square through
Row 6.

STITCH GUIDE
POPCORN (uses one dc)
4 Dc in dc indicated, drop
loop from hook, insert hook
in first dc of 4-dc group, hook
loop and draw through st,
ch 1 to close.
PICOT
Ch 4, slip st in top of last sc
made.

FIRST SQUARE
Ch 6; join with slip st to form a
ring **(beginning ring made)**.

Row 1: Ch 3 **(counts as first
dc, now and throughout)**,
(dc in ring, ch 3) twice, 2 dc in
ring: 5 dc and 2 ch-3 sps.

Row 2 (Right side)**:** Ch 3, turn;
dc in next dc, ch 3, 3 dc in next
dc, ch 3, dc in last 2 dc: 7 dc
and 2 ch-3 sps.

Note: Loop a short piece of
yarn around any stitch to mark
Row 2 as **right** side.

Row 3: Ch 3, turn; dc in next
dc, ch 3, 2 dc in next dc, ch 3,
skip next dc, 2 dc in next dc,
ch 3, dc in last 2 dc: 8 dc and
3 ch-3 sps.

Row 4: Ch 3, turn; dc in next
dc, ch 3, dc in next dc, work
Popcorn in next dc, (2 dc, ch 3,
2 dc) in next ch-3 sp, work
Popcorn in next dc, dc in next
dc, ch 3, dc in last 2 dc: 10 dc,
2 Popcorns, and 3 ch-3 sps.

Instructions continued on page 26.

Row 5: Ch 3, turn; dc in next dc, ch 3, dc in next dc, skip closing ch of next Popcorn, dc in Popcorn and in next 2 dc, (2 dc, ch 3, 2 dc) in next ch-3 sp, dc in next 2 dc, skip closing ch of next Popcorn, dc in Popcorn and in next dc, ch 3, dc in last 2 dc: 16 dc and 3 ch-3 sps.

Row 6: Ch 3, turn; dc in next dc, ch 3, dc in next dc, work Popcorn in next dc, dc in next 3 dc, work Popcorn in next dc, (2 dc, ch 3, 2 dc) in next ch-3 sp, work Popcorn in next dc, dc in next 3 dc, work Popcorn in next dc, dc in next dc, ch 3, dc in last 2 dc: 16 dc, 4 Popcorns, and 3 ch-3 sps.

Row 7: Ch 3, turn; dc in next dc, ch 3, dc in next dc, skip closing ch of next Popcorn, dc in Popcorn and in next 3 dc, skip closing ch of next Popcorn, dc in Popcorn and in next 2 dc, (2 dc, ch 3, 2 dc) in next ch-3 sp, dc in next 2 dc, skip closing ch of next Popcorn, dc in Popcorn and in next 3 dc, skip closing ch of next Popcorn, dc in Popcorn and in next dc, ch 3, dc in last 2 dc: 24 dc and 3 ch-3 sps.

Row 8: Ch 3, turn; dc in next dc, ch 3, dc in next dc, work Popcorn in next dc, (dc in next 3 dc, work Popcorn in next dc) twice, (2 dc, ch 3, 2 dc) in next ch-3 sp, work Popcorn in next dc, (dc in next 3 dc, work Popcorn in next dc) twice, dc in next dc, ch 3, dc in last 2 dc: 22 dc, 6 Popcorns, and 3 ch-3 sps.

Row 9: Ch 3, turn; dc in next dc, ch 3, dc in next dc, (skip closing ch of next Popcorn, dc in Popcorn and in next 3 dc) twice, skip closing ch of next Popcorn, dc in Popcorn and in next 2 dc, (2 dc, ch 3, 2 dc) in next ch-3 sp, dc in next 2 dc, (skip closing ch of next Popcorn, dc in Popcorn and in next 3 dc) twice, skip closing ch of next Popcorn, dc in Popcorn and in next dc, ch 3, dc in last 2 dc: 32 dc and 3 ch-3 sps.

Row 10: Ch 3, turn; dc in next dc, ch 3, dc in next dc, work Popcorn in next dc, (dc in next 3 dc, work Popcorn in next dc) 3 times, (2 dc, ch 3, 2 dc) in next ch-3 sp, work Popcorn in next dc, (dc in next 3 dc, work Popcorn in next dc) 3 times, dc in next dc, ch 3, dc in last 2 dc: 28 dc, 8 Popcorns, and 3 ch-3 sps.

Row 11: Ch 3, turn; dc in next dc, ch 3, dc in next dc, (skip closing ch of next Popcorn, dc in Popcorn and in next 3 dc) 3 times, skip closing ch of next Popcorn, dc in Popcorn and in next 2 dc, (2 dc, ch 3, 2 dc) in next ch-3 sp, dc in next 2 dc, (skip closing ch of next Popcorn, dc in Popcorn and in next 3 dc) 3 times, skip closing ch of next Popcorn, dc in Popcorn and in next dc, ch 3, dc in last 2 dc: 40 dc and 3 ch-3 sps.

Row 12: Ch 3, turn; dc in next dc, ch 3, dc in next dc, work Popcorn in next dc, (dc in next 3 dc, work Popcorn in next dc) 4 times, (2 dc, ch 3, 2 dc) in next ch-3 sp, work Popcorn in next dc, (dc in next 3 dc, work Popcorn in next dc) 4 times, dc in next dc, ch 3, dc in last 2 dc: 34 dc, 10 Popcorns, and 3 ch-3 sps.

Row 13: Ch 3, turn; dc in next dc, ch 3, dc in next dc, (skip closing ch of next Popcorn, dc in Popcorn and in next 3 dc) 4 times, skip closing ch of next Popcorn, dc in Popcorn and in next 2 dc, (2 dc, ch 3, 2 dc) in next ch-3 sp, dc in next 2 dc, (skip closing ch of next Popcorn, dc in Popcorn and in next 3 dc) 4 times, skip closing ch of next Popcorn, dc in Popcorn and in next dc, ch 3, dc in last 2 dc: 48 dc and 3 ch-3 sps.

Row 14: Ch 3, turn; dc in next dc, ch 3, dc in next dc, work Popcorn in next dc, (dc in next 3 dc, work Popcorn in next dc) 5 times, (2 dc, ch 3, 2 dc) in next ch-3 sp, work Popcorn in next dc, (dc in next 3 dc, work Popcorn in next dc) 5 times, dc in next dc, ch 3, dc in last 2 dc: 40 dc, 12 Popcorns, and 3 ch-3 sps.

Row 15: Ch 3, turn; dc in next dc, ch 3, dc in next dc, (skip closing ch of next Popcorn, dc in Popcorn and in next 3 dc) 5 times, skip closing ch of next Popcorn, dc in Popcorn and in next 2 dc, (2 dc, ch 3, 2 dc) in next ch-3 sp, dc in next 2 dc, (skip closing ch of next Popcorn, dc in Popcorn and in next 3 dc) 5 times, skip closing ch of next Popcorn, dc in Popcorn and in next dc, ch 3, dc in last 2 dc: 56 dc and 3 ch-3 sps.

Instructions continued on page 28.

Edging Rnd: Ch 1, turn; sc in first 2 dc and in next ch, work Picot, sc in next 2 chs and in next dc, work Picot, (sc in next 3 dc, work Picot) 8 times, sc in next dc, 2 sc in next ch-3 sp, work Picot, 2 sc in same ch-3 sp, sc in next dc, work Picot, (sc in next 3 dc, work Picot) 8 times, sc in next dc and in next 2 chs, work Picot, sc in next ch and in last 2 dc, work Picot, sc in last dc; working in end of rows, 2 sc in first row, work Picot, 2 sc in next row, sc in next row, work Picot, sc in same row, (2 sc in next row, work Picot, 2 sc in next row, sc in next row, work Picot, sc in same row) 4 times, (2 sc, work Picot, 2 sc) in beginning ring; working in end of rows, sc in first row, work Picot, sc in same row, 2 sc in next row, work Picot, 2 sc in next row, (sc in next row, work Picot, sc in same row, 2 sc in next row, work Picot, 2 sc in next row) 4 times, sc in same st as first sc, work Picot; join with slip st to first sc, finish off: 10 Picots on **each** side and 4 corner Picots.

SECOND SQUARE

Note: The method used to connect the Squares is a no-sew joining also known as "join-as-you-go". After the First Square is made, each remaining Square is worked through Row 15, then crocheted together as the Edging Rnd is worked. Refer to the Placement Diagram as a guide for proper placement of beginning ring.

Work same as First Square through Row 15: 56 dc and 3 ch-3 sps.

Edging Rnd: Ch 1, turn; sc in first 2 dc and in next ch, work Picot, sc in next 2 chs and in next dc, work Picot, (sc in next 3 dc, work Picot) 8 times, sc in next dc, 2 sc in next ch-3 sp, work Picot, 2 sc in same ch-3 sp, sc in next dc, work Picot, (sc in next 3 dc, work Picot) 8 times, sc in next dc and in next 2 chs, work Picot, sc in next ch and in last 2 dc, work Picot, sc in last dc; working in end of rows, 2 sc in first row, work Picot, 2 sc in next row, sc in next row, work Picot, sc in same row, (2 sc in next row, work Picot, 2 sc in next row, sc in next row, work Picot, sc in same row) 4 times, 2 sc in beginning ring, ch 2, holding Squares with **wrong** sides together, slip st in corresponding corner Picot on **First Square**, ch 2, slip st in top of last sc made on **Second Square**, 2 sc in beginning ring, working in end of rows, sc in first row, ch 2, slip st in next Picot on **First Square**, ch 2, slip st in top of last sc made on **Second Square**, sc in same row, 2 sc in next row, ch 2, slip st in next Picot on **First Square**, ch 2, slip st in top of last sc made on **Second Square**, 2 sc in next row, [sc in next row, ch 2, slip st in next Picot on **First Square**, ch 2, slip st in top of last sc made on **Second Square**, sc in same row, 2 sc in next row, ch 2, slip st in next Picot on **First Square**, ch 2, slip st in top of last sc made on **Second Square**, 2 sc in next row] 4 times, sc in same st as first sc, ch 2, slip st in next corner Picot on **First Square**, ch 2, slip st in top of last sc made; join with slip st to first sc, finish off.

Referring to Placement Diagram for correct placement of beginning ring, work remaining Squares in same manner as Second Square, joining to adjacent square(s) when necessary (if a corner was previously joined, slip st in joining slip st).

Design by Kim Kotary.

PLACEMENT DIAGRAM

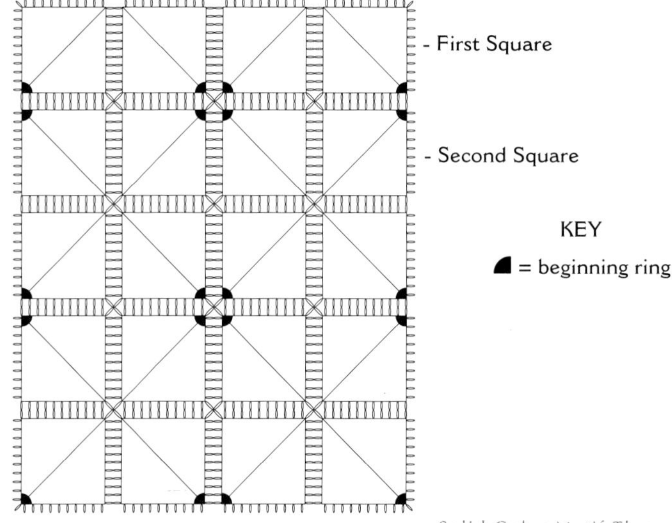

GENERAL INSTRUCTIONS

ABBREVIATIONS

ch(s)	chain(s)	Rnd(s)	Round(s)
cm	centimeters	sc	single crochet(s)
dc	double crochet(s)	sp(s)	space(s)
dtr	double treble crochet(s)	st(s)	stitch(es)
hdc	half double crochet(s)	tr	treble crochet(s)
MC	Main Color	YO	yarn over

★ — work instructions following ★ as many **more** times as indicated in addition to the first time.

† to † or ♥ to ♥ — work all instructions from first † to second † or from first ♥ to second ♥ **as many** times as specified.

( ) or [ ] — work enclosed instructions as many times as specified by the number immediately following **or** work all enclosed instructions in the stitch or space indicated **or** contains explanatory remarks.

colon (:) — the number(s) given after a colon at the end of a row or round denote(s) the number of stitches or spaces you should have on that row or round.

CROCHET TERMINOLOGY		
UNITED STATES		**INTERNATIONAL**
slip stitch (slip st)	=	single crochet (sc)
single crochet (sc)	=	double crochet (dc)
half double crochet (hdc)	=	half treble crochet (htr)
double crochet (dc)	=	treble crochet(tr)
treble crochet (tr)	=	double treble crochet (dtr)
double treble crochet (dtr)	=	triple treble crochet (ttr)
triple treble crochet (tr tr)	=	quadruple treble crochet (qtr)
skip	=	miss

◼☐☐☐ **BEGINNER**	Projects for first-time crocheters using basic stitches. Minimal shaping.
◼◼☐☐ **EASY**	Projects using yarn with basic stitches, repetitive stitch patterns, simple color changes, and simple shaping and finishing.
◼◼◼☐ **INTERMEDIATE**	Projects using a variety of techniques, such as basic lace patterns or color patterns, mid-level shaping and finishing.
◼◼◼◼ **EXPERIENCED**	Projects with intricate stitch patterns, techniques and dimension, such as non-repeating patterns, multi-color techniques, fine threads, small hooks, detailed shaping and refined finishing.

GAUGE

Exact gauge is essential for proper size. Before beginning your project, make the sample swatch given in the individual instructions in the yarn and hook specified. After completing the swatch, measure it, counting your stitches and rows or rounds carefully. If your swatch is larger or smaller than specified, **make another, changing hook size to get the correct gauge**. Keep trying until you find the size hook that will give you the specified gauge.

HINTS

As in all crocheted pieces, good finishing techniques make a big difference in the quality of the piece. Make a habit of taking care of loose ends as you work. Thread a yarn needle with the yarn end. With **wrong** side facing, weave the needle through several stitches, then reverse the direction and weave it back through several stitches. When ends are secure, clip them off close to work.

CROCHET HOOKS	
Metric mm	**U.S.**
2.25	B-1
2.75	C-2
3.25	D-3
3.5	E-4
3.75	F-5
4	G-6
5	H-8
5.5	I-9
6	J-10
6.5	K-10½
9	N
10	P
15	Q

Yarn Weight Symbol & Names	LACE 0	SUPER FINE 1	FINE 2	LIGHT 3	MEDIUM 4	BULKY 5	SUPER BULKY 6
Type of Yarns in Category	Fingering, 10-count crochet thread	Sock, Fingering Baby	Sport, Baby	DK, Light Worsted	Worsted, Afghan, Aran	Chunky, Craft, Rug	Bulky, Roving
Crochet Gauge* Ranges in Single Crochet to 4" (10 cm)	32-42 double crochets**	21-32 sts	16-20 sts	12-17 sts	11-14 sts	8-11 sts	5-9 sts
Advised Hook Size Range	Steel*** 6,7,8 Regular hook B-1	B-1 to E-4	E-4 to 7	7 to I-9	I-9 to K-10.5	K-10.5 to M-13	M-13 and larger

*GUIDELINES ONLY: The chart above reflects the most commonly used gauges and hook sizes for specific yarn categories.

** Lace weight yarns are usually crocheted on larger-size hooks to create lacy openwork patterns. Accordingly, a gauge range is difficult to determine. Always follow the gauge stated in your pattern.

*** Steel crochet hooks are sized differently from regular hooks–the higher the number the smaller the hook, which is the reverse of regular hook sizing.

JOINING WITH SC

When instructed to join with sc, begin with a slip knot on hook. Insert hook in stitch or space indicated, YO and pull up a loop, YO and draw through both loops on hook.

JOINING WITH DC

When instructed to join with dc, begin with a slip knot on the hook. YO, holding loop on hook, insert hook in stitch or space indicated, YO and pull up a loop (3 loops on hook), (YO and draw through 2 loops on hook) twice.

BACK LOOP ONLY

Work only in loop(s) indicated by arrow *(Fig. 1)*.

Fig. 1

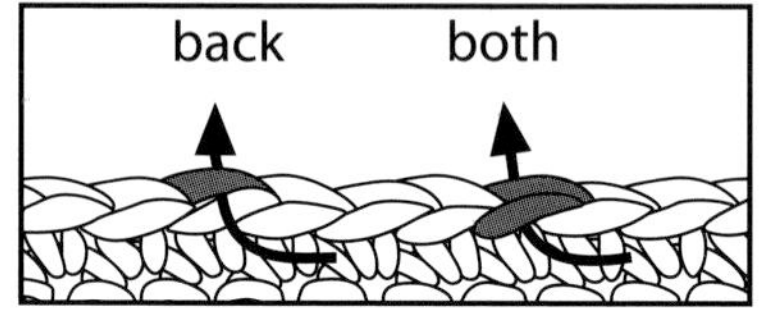

REVERSE SINGLE CROCHET

Working from **left** to **right**, ★ insert hook in the stitch to the right of the hook *(Fig. 2a)*, YO and draw through, under and to the left of the loop on the hook (2 loops on hook) *(Fig. 2b)*, YO and draw through both loops on hook *(Fig. 2c)* (**reverse sc made**, *Fig. 2d*); repeat from ★ around.

Fig. 2a

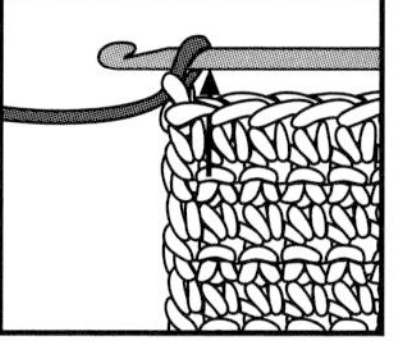

Fig. 2b

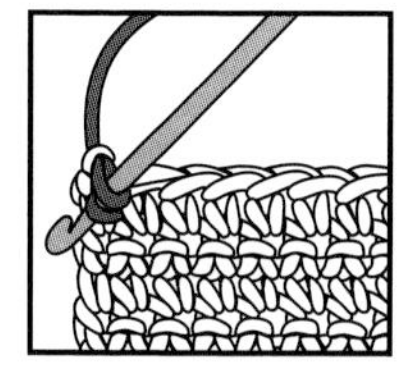

Fig. 2c

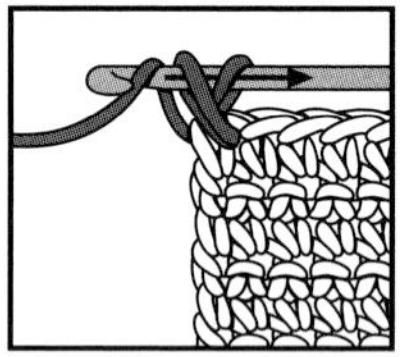

Fig. 2d

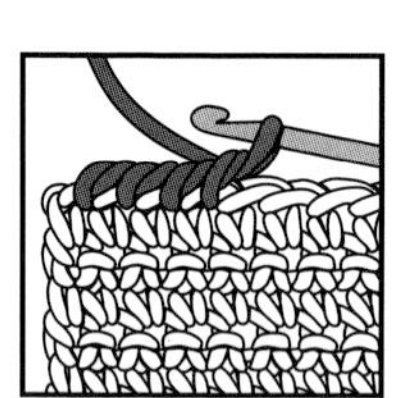

We have made every effort to ensure that these instructions are accurate and complete. We cannot, however, be responsible for human error, typographical mistakes, or variations in individual work.